Path of the Pronghorn

Cat Urbigkit

Photographs by
Mark Gocke

BOYDS MILLS PRESS
Honesdale, Pennsylvania

The author wishes to thank Richard E. McCabe,
executive vice president of the Wildlife Management Institute, Washington, D.C.,
for his gracious assistance.

CIP data is available.

Boyds Mills Press, Inc.
815 Church Street
Honesdale, Pennsylvania 18431
Printed in the United States of America

First edition
The text of this book is set in 14-point Minion.

10 9 8 7 6 5 4 3 2 1

To Arlo Bean
—*C.U.*

To my children, Jonah and Emilie,
in hope that they may be able to witness the
annual migration of the pronghorn throughout their lifetime
—*M.G.*

*(left) A fawn needs her mother's milk.
(below) Fawns hide by lying still on the ground until they are strong enough to run away from predators.*

I<small>T IS SPRINGTIME IN</small> W<small>YOMING.</small>

Tucked into a small opening amid a sea of sagebrush on the Wyoming steppe, a pronghorn antelope doe gives birth to a tiny fawn. The doe is one of a small group that has left the much larger Sublette herd of Sublette County to find a quiet place as fawning time approaches. Each doe then finds her own spot to give birth, away from the others. Female pronghorn have one or two fawns, and sometimes triplets.

A seven-pound fawn peers out into the world through large eyes. It stands on long, shaky legs to drink its mother's milk. The doe gently licks the nursing fawn. The fawn's big eyes will enable it to spot trouble from a long distance, while its long legs will soon allow it to run from danger.

But for now, the fawn hides. For the first few weeks of life, pronghorn fawns will spend much time hiding, until they are strong enough to outrun predators that might try to kill and eat them.

When danger appears, a doe will leave her fawns hidden as she runs away, drawing the predator toward her and away from her babies. The doe may even attack a predator, striking with her front feet, to defend her fawns against a coyote or an eagle.

When the doe returns to find her baby, the doe makes clicking noises as she searches the brush for her fawn. The fawn stands to greet its mother.

Golden Eagle

A doe is ready to protect her fawn from predators.

Fawns are born on this treeless range, which is called a steppe, or a sagebrush desert. Sagebrush, grasses, and other brush and vegetation hold plenty of nutrition for the animals that spend their winter and spring here, where the snows are not too deep.

Fawns start running when just a few days old, dashing around their mothers at speeds up to twenty-five miles an hour! As fawns mature, they will run even faster.

Coyote

Although it's called the American pronghorn antelope, this animal isn't an antelope at all. The pronghorn may resemble African antelope, but they actually have no close relative.

The doe and other adult pronghorn can run for short distances at nearly sixty miles per hour and for several miles at speeds exceeding thirty miles per hour.

Pronghorn are the fastest land mammals in North America. Of all the world's land mammals, only the cheetah, clocked at speeds of up to seventy miles per hour, is faster.

Pronghorn are smaller than elk or deer. Unlike these animals, pronghorn do not have dewclaws, which could affect their speed. A dewclaw is a toe-like hoof located above the main hoof, as shown in this photograph of an elk foot. When an animal is standing on a firm surface, its dewclaws do not touch the ground. But these dewclaws may come in contact with the ground when the animal is running or traveling through snow, which could slow them down.

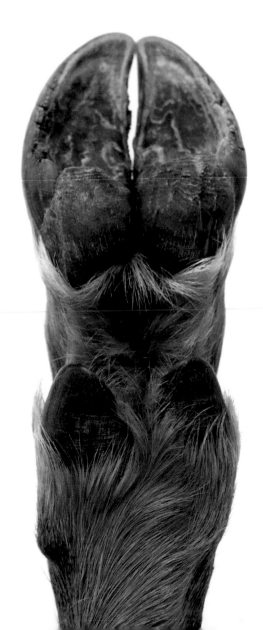

Scientists believe that thousands of years ago, a cheetah-like animal inhabited North America. Pronghorn may have evolved into fast runners, with small but strong bones, long limbs, and big heart and lungs, as a result of these predators. When a pronghorn senses danger, a powerful instinct causes it to burst into a run.

A few weeks after having their babies, pronghorn does and their fawns once again form small groups. These groups meet and mix, and travel together in spring migrations. They head for higher elevations in the mountains and foothills, where they will spend the summer, taking advantage of lush vegetation the melting winter snows have left behind.

Since pronghorn are social animals, they spend almost all of their time with other pronghorn. During the day, pronghorn fawns often come together in small "nursery" groups that are supervised by one or two does, while the other mothers are off feeding.

The does and fawns make bleating sounds, calling to each other. Adult pronghorn also make other vocalizations—they snort, blow, and bark when alarmed.

The fast-growing young pronghorn are very active, running, sparring, and butting each other. They are cautious creatures, but at the same time curious and playful.

The pronghorn's scientific name is Antilocapra americana. Antilo *means "antelope," and* capra *means "goat." Antilocapra americana translates into "the antelope-goat of America."*

Adult male pronghorn, called bucks, will often travel together or join groups of does with fawns. The bucks have prong-shaped bony horns that are covered by horn sheaths. The black-colored sheaths are hollow and made up of a stiff, hair-like substance.

Many does also have horns, but these are much smaller than those grown by bucks. Bucks shed the outer layer of their horns every year, usually late in the fall, but does shed their sheaths only about every two to five years. Pronghorn antelope are the only hoofed animal in the world to shed their horn sheaths.

Bucks have large horns.

Pronghorn, cattle, camels, and giraffes are mammals called ruminants. These animals perform a remarkable feat. They live on plants that most other mammals can't digest.

How do ruminants get the nutrition they need from low-nutrient plants? After all, if they couldn't do that, they could not survive where they live.

The answer is the ruminant stomach. Unlike the one-chambered stomach in humans, the stomach of a ruminant may have three or four chambers. (Pronghorn have four.) Here's how this kind of stomach works.

As a pronghorn eats, it chews its food a little before swallowing it into the first two chambers of the stomach. These chambers separate the food into layers of liquid and solids. The solids form clumps called cuds, which the animal later burps back into its mouth for further chewing. Ruminants are well known for lying still for long periods while chewing their cuds.

The saliva produced during the pronghorn's chewing and grinding helps break the food into even smaller pieces, which are then swallowed into the next chamber of the stomach. Here, microorganisms feed on the tough plant material (cellulose), breaking it down into sugars and carbohydrates that the body can use. The microorganisms grow and multiply as they feed, building proteins for their own growth.

The last chamber is much like the human stomach. There, digestive juices kill the microorganisms and break down the proteins. In the intestines, the nutrients are absorbed into the bloodstream.

Adult pronghorn rarely weigh more than 120 pounds, making pronghorn the smallest ruminant game animal in North America.

Does have small horns.

13

After spending summer in the mountainous high country, the herds move back toward lower-elevation winter range. They sense when to go by the change of the season to autumn, with its early snowfall, followed by warm, sunny days.

When it's time to migrate, a pronghorn herd doesn't simply meander down the trail, taking it easy and snacking along the way. Much of the route is taken at a run, with the migration lasting only a few days.

When a herd of pronghorn passes by at a run,
it sounds like a wildfire raging across the prairie.
But there is no fire. The sound comes from hundreds
of pounding hooves striking the hard-packed ground,
kicking up dust in their wake.

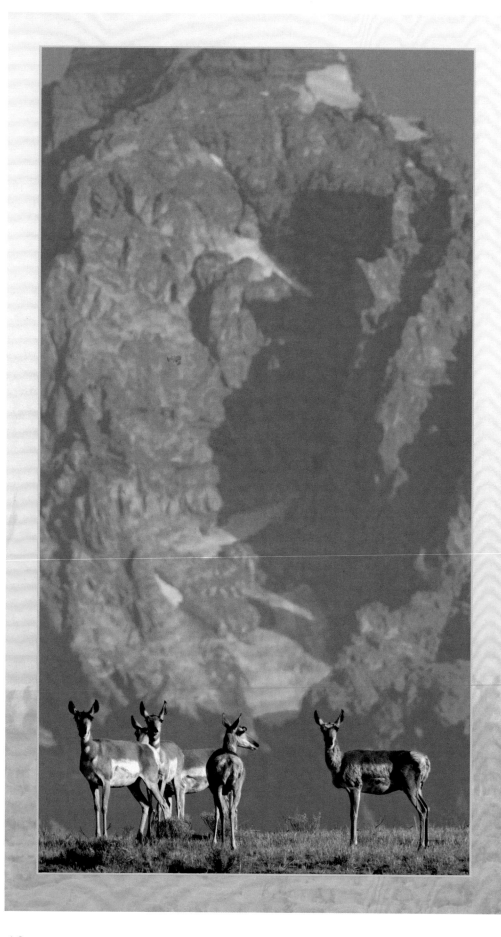

These pronghorn are members of the Sublette herd of Sublette County in western Wyoming. The herd participates in the longest land-mammal migration in the continental United States. It's a seasonal movement that has taken place since the last Ice Age, about ten thousand years ago.

Following the melting snow and warmer temperatures, this herd moves from low-elevation winter range in the sagebrush desert, to summer range in mountain valleys. The animals travel up to two hundred miles to spend the summer in Grand Teton National Park. When fall arrives, the animals hit the return trail. By migrating with the seasons, the animals take advantage of the best feeding opportunities.

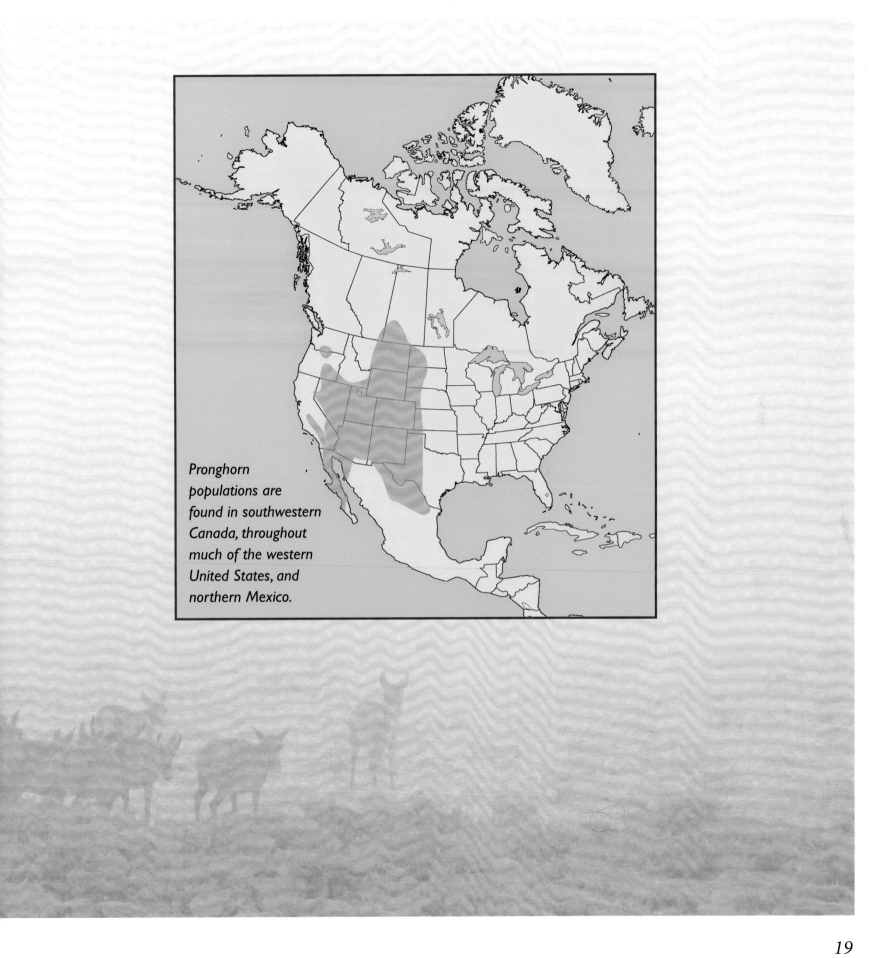

Pronghorn populations are found in southwestern Canada, throughout much of the western United States, and northern Mexico.

Green River

Gros Ventre Mountains

Duck Creek

Part of this migration involves travel through the Trappers Point bottleneck. Trappers Point is an area near Pinedale, Wyoming. It is called a bottleneck because two rivers border the one-mile-wide swath of open land, creating a geographic bottleneck in the pronghorn migration path. Human development has narrowed the bottleneck further, so the herd is funneled into a pathway about a half-mile wide.

Bones unearthed at Trappers Point reveal that this pronghorn migration route was in use six thousand years ago. The doe and her fawn from the Sublette herd follow this ancient path, as hundreds of thousands of pronghorn have done before them.

(left) *The Green River, on the left, and Duck Creek, on the upper right, form a natural passageway known as the Trappers Point migration bottleneck. The photo shows the view looking northwest, with the Gros Ventre Mountains in the far distance.*

When the group of pronghorn runs, the contrasting tan and white colors on their bodies seem to blend together, making it difficult to identify single animals. This serves as a defense against predators.

Pronghorn have short manes and large white rump patches. When alarmed, pronghorn erect the hair on their manes or rumps, a visible warning sign to other herd members.

It may seem like all pronghorn look alike, but that's not true. They each have their own coat colors, markings, and horn shapes and sizes. The white-colored hair on the brown neck is called a neckband, and it aids in identification of individual pronghorn when they aren't running.

Bucks can be identified by black cheek patches located just below their ears. The cheek patches cover scent glands and vary in size with the season. During late summer's breeding season, called rut, the patches swell to about twice their normal size.

Pronghorn bucks fight for breeding rights during rut, sometimes doing battle horn-to-horn. During rut, bucks are easy to identify with their swollen necks, glands, and patches. They often rub their horns in the brush and sometimes roam with vegetation hanging from their horns.

A breeding buck will work to gather a harem of does and their fawns. The buck will try to keep other bucks from mating with his group of does or will defend his breeding territory. Bucks are very aggressive during rut and will often chase each other during this time.

As vegetation dries out in the late summer heat, the herd moves onto ranchlands to find freshly mown hayfields, a source of good nutrition.

As they rest during the day, the animals regurgitate food, called cud, back into their mouths. Chewing the cud provides for full and better digestion.

Once rut is over and the winter season begins, pronghorn bands move again, leaving the mountains or higher elevations for their winter range below. As snow gets deeper, the size of the pronghorn herd grows bigger as more animals come together. Does and fawns blend into the herd.

The animals move together, their hooves breaking through the snow to reveal vegetation underneath. Pronghorn paw the snow away from brush so they can nibble leaves and plants. If you could smell a pronghorn's breath after it has eaten, you might inhale the sweet smell of sagebrush.

The hair on a pronghorn helps the animal survive extremely cold winter temperatures. Pronghorn hair is hollow, providing excellent insulation from the cold.

As snowmelt hints of the coming spring, pronghorn begin to break into smaller groups. Once again, they are ready to travel the ancient migration trail, as did their ancestors thousands of years before.

Last year's fawns are now adults and move with the rest of the herd as it follows the path of the pronghorn.

More about Pronghorn

Since pronghorn are migratory animals, human activity, such as development, can pose a threat to their migratory trail. Unlike most big-game species, pronghorn typically crawl under fences rather than jump over. Many ranchers construct or modify fences so that the bottom wire is high enough off the ground to allow pronghorn to get through.

Two hundred years ago, there were millions of pronghorn. But within the past century, pronghorn numbers plunged, sending the species to near extinction. By the 1920s, unregulated hunting, drought, and construction in previously undisturbed habitat resulted in fewer than twelve thousand pronghorn across the entire range of the species. Many people thought the pronghorn was sure to become extinct.

Conservation measures and the elimination of hunting seasons soon resulted in population increases. Today, more than a million pronghorn are spread across the western range of the United States, southern Canada, and portions of Mexico—so many that regulated hunting is again allowed over most of the pronghorn's range.

Wyoming has the largest pronghorn population in the United States, including the Sublette herd. From a low of only 2,000 animals in 1906, the state's population increased to 150,000 in 1963 and to more than 515,000 in 2007. The pronghorn that live in the hot desert of the southwestern United States and Mexico are uniquely suited for this habitat, but only about 1,000 of the animals remain there.

In 2008, the United States Forest Service established the nation's first designated wildlife migration route. This Pronghorn Migration Corridor is located in western Wyoming. The official designation protects a major portion of the ancient pronghorn migration trail from development, ensuring that migrations will continue for years to come.

Sources

Arizona Game and Fish Department. Unpublished abstract compiled and edited by the Heritage Data Management System, Arizona Game and Fish Department, Phoenix, AZ, 2007.

Berger, Kim M., John P. Beckmann, and Joel Berger. "Wildlife and Energy Development: Pronghorn of the Upper Green River Basin—Year 2 Summary." New York: Wildlife Conservation Society, 2007.

Burt, William H., and Richard P. Grossenheider. *A Field Guide to the Mammals of North America North of Mexico.* 3rd ed. A Peterson Field Guide. Boston: Houghton Mifflin, 1976.

Byers, John A. *American Pronghorn: Social Adaptations and Ghosts of Predators Past.* Chicago: University of Chicago Press, 1997.

Byers, John A. *Built for Speed: A Year in the Life of Pronghorn.* Cambridge, MA: Harvard University Press, 2003.

McCabe, Richard E., Bart W. O'Gara, and Henry M. Reeves. *Prairie Ghost: Pronghorn and Human Interaction in Early America.* Boulder: University Press of Colorado, 2004.

O'Gara, Bart, and James D. Yoakum. *Pronghorn: Ecology and Management.* Boulder: University Press of Colorado, 2004.

Sawyer, Hall, and Fred Lindzey. "The Jackson Hole Pronghorn Study." Laramie: Wyoming Cooperative Fish and Wildlife Research Unit, University of Wyoming, 2000.

Sawyer, Hall, Fred Lindzey, and Doug McWhirter. "Mule Deer and Pronghorn Migration in Western Wyoming." *Wildlife Society Bulletin* (2005) 33: 1266–1273.